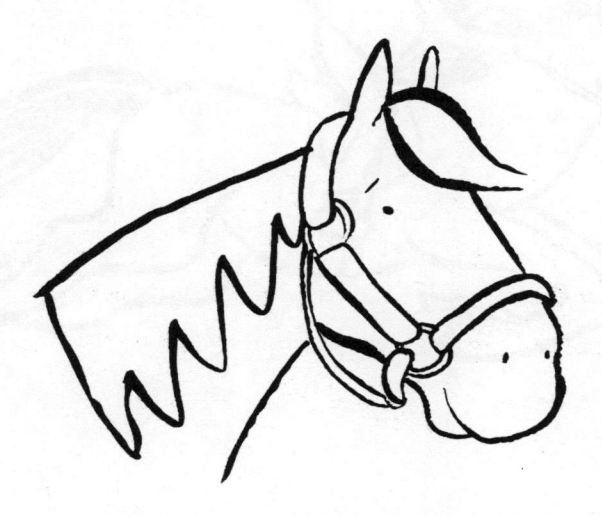

My Pony Handbook

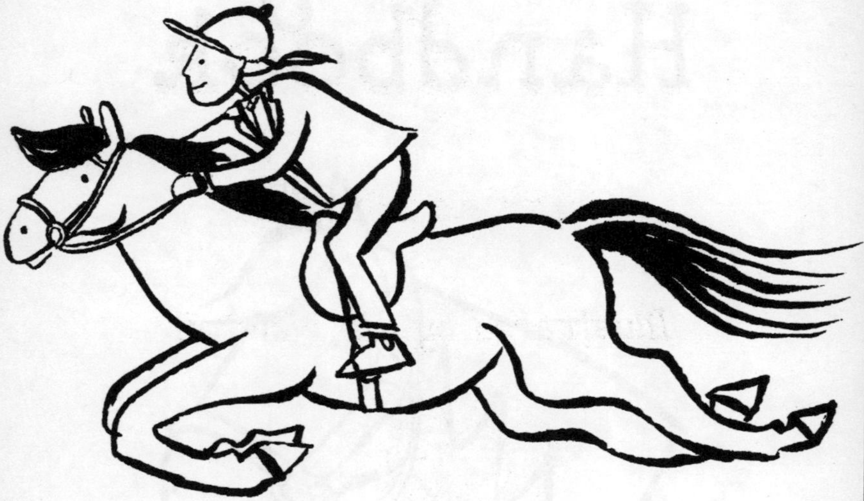

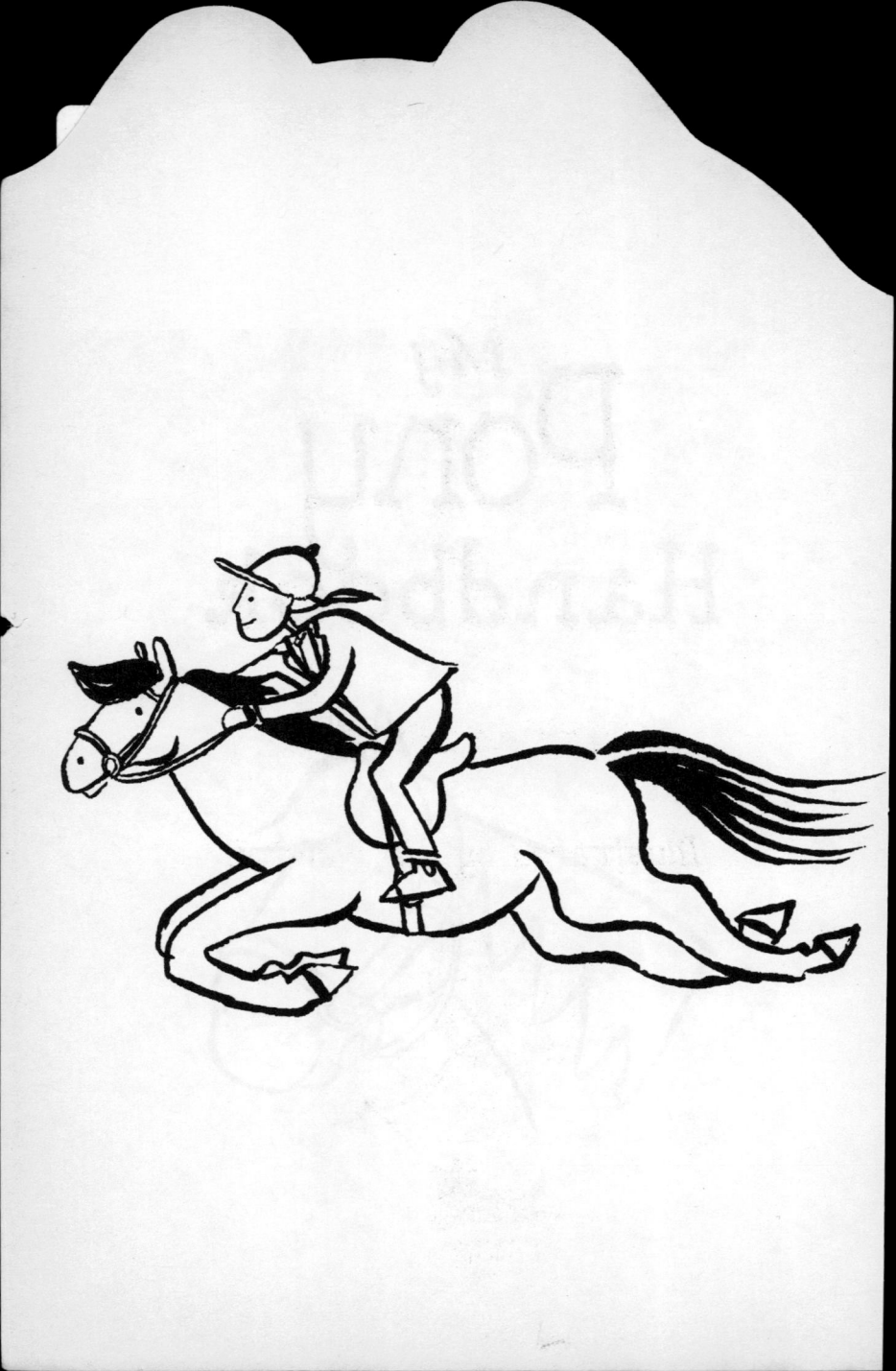

My Pony Handbook

Caroline Plaisted

Illustrated by Jill Newton

BLOOMSBURY
CHILDREN'S
BOOKS

With thanks to Jessica Middleton, British Show Pony Society and Ponies UK judge, for checking this book and for so much more

All rights reserved; no part of this publication may be reproduced or transmitted by any means, electronic, mechanical, photocopying or otherwise, without the prior permission of the publisher

First published in Great Britain in 1999
Bloomsbury Publishing Plc, 38 Soho Square, London, W1V 5DF

Copyright © Text Caroline Plaisted 1999
Copyright © Illustrations Jill Newton 1999

The moral right of the author has been asserted
A CIP catalogue record of this book is available from the British Library

ISBN 0 7475 4402 6

Printed in England by Clays Ltd, St Ives plc

10 9 8 7 6 5 4 3 2 1

Contents

Introduction	7
Pony breeds	9
What to wear to ride	14
Tackle that tack!	18
How to mount a pony	22
Trot on!	25
Where to go for riding lessons	28
What to feed a pony	30
Grooming your pony	35
Mucking out and stable stuff	40
The Pony Club	43
Riding etiquette	47
Top riding tips	52
Gymkhanas and shows	56

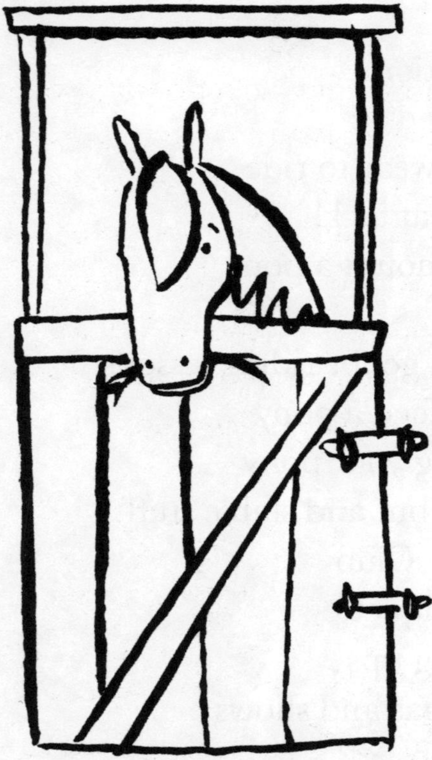

Introduction

The more you learn about ponies, the more you will know that every gorgeous little pony has a character of its own. And every cute little pony is waiting for you to be its best friend!

Even if you aren't lucky enough to own a pony of your own, there is still a lot you can learn about ponies: from tips on how to ride, what you should and shouldn't feed a pony, and on to how to make a pony warm and comfortable both out riding and in a stable.

If you don't already have riding lessons, why not practise your riding technique on a rocking horse? Did you know that the first rocking horses were originally made so that people could learn to ride before they got on to a real pony? If you don't know someone with a rocking horse, you could still practise your riding on the arm of a chair.

What are you waiting for? Trot on!

Pony breeds

It could be that the pony you love is a crossbreed or a mixture of several breeds rather than a thoroughbred. (Just like some dogs are mongrels rather than pedigrees.) But each breed of pony has its own characteristics and it's useful for all riders to know which pony is which.

Connemara
These are natural jumpers and are known for their reliability and toughness. They are usually dun-coloured or grey.

Dale

These tough ponies have been known to be strong enough to carry a farmer all day in the fell country where they come from. They are quiet, powerful and neat and are very popular for pony-trekking. Colours are bay, black, brown and grey.

Dartmoor

These make ideal first ponies and they are usually bay, black or brown in colour. They are known for being kind and placid.

Exmoor

Another well-mannered pony, Exmoors are strong and have thick, wiry winter coats. They have a unique "mealy" or oatmeal-coloured muzzle.

Fell

Very similar to the Dale pony but slightly smaller. They are popular for pony-trekking.

Highland

These are strong and agile ponies. They are valued for their strength and their reliability. Many of them are found in shades of dun but they are also known to be grey, bay, dark brown and chestnut.

New Forest

These ponies are quick to learn and particularly love taking part in sporting events like the Pony Club rallies (see pages 43-46 for more information about the Pony Club). Some New Forest ponies are big enough for adults to ride them.

Shetland

The smallest of the native breeds of ponies but for their size they are the strongest. They are well-known for their thick manes and tail hair as well as their very thick coats. They may be piebald or skewbald in colour as well as any of the whole colours.

Welsh Mountain

These adaptable ponies are known for having very intelligent-looking faces. They are gentle and courageous companions. Welsh Mountain ponies are divided into four sizes (A,B,C and D). Those from Section A are usually the first ones you would ride.

What to wear to ride

When you ride your pony you will need to wear special clothes which will look smart, be comfortable and keep you protected. You will wear different clothes depending on the weather or if you are taking part in a show or gymkhana (see pages 56-64 for more information about these).

A waxed waterproof riding coat will keep you warm and dry.

A crash helmet has no peak and may be covered with a colourful silk. Make sure that your hat reaches the British Safety Standards recommended.

A hard hat has a peak and is usually covered with velvet for shows and gymkhanas. All riding hats should be properly fitted and strapped tightly under the chin.

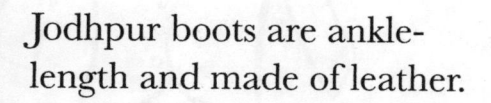

Jodhpur boots are ankle-length and made of leather.

Long boots are made of leather or rubber.

Jodhpurs are ankle-length and have padding on the inside of the knees to protect them from rubbing against the saddle.

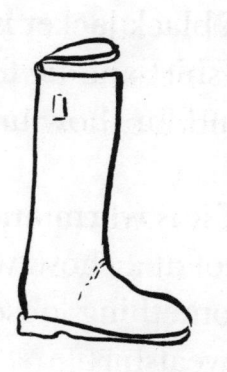

A white shirt and tie
(usually a Pony Club one) is
worn for a show.

A tweed jacket known as a
hacking jacket is worn for
gymkhanas and some show
classes.

A black jacket is worn with
a shirt and tie for a show
and for showjumping.

If it is warm and you are
not at a show, wear
something loose like a
sweatshirt.

Hair should be neat and tidy. Keep it cut short, tie it back or wear a hairnet if you are competing in a show and need to look very smart.

Wear gloves with a special bobbly surface that helps you to grip the reins.

A body protector is worn on top of your everyday clothes or underneath a show jacket and will protect you if you fall off.

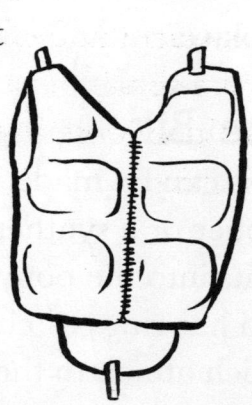

Tackle that tack!

It is just as important for your pony to wear the right things as you. If your pony is properly tacked up he will be comfortable and so will you!

The Bridle
This is made of leather or fabric and fits over the pony's head. It holds the Bit in place.

The Bit
This can be made of metal or rubber or a synthetic material. It fits into the pony's mouth and has rings or cheek pieces which attach to the Bridle.

The Reins
These are attached to either side of the Bit.

Headcollars
When you are not riding a pony, you still need to be able to control it so that you can catch it, put it into a pony box or stable it. A headcollar can be made of nylon or leather. A lead rope attaches to the ring on the headcollar.

The Saddle
This must be fitted to both the pony and the rider. The padded panels underneath the saddle protect the pony's spine. The front of the saddle is called the pommel. The cantle

is the highest part at the back of the saddle. The deepest part of the saddle is the seat where the rider should sit. The girth is attached to either side of the saddle and goes under the pony's stomach. It keeps the saddle in place.

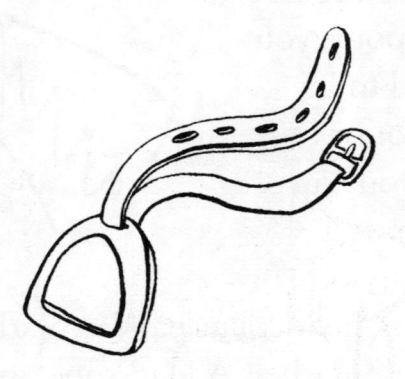

Stirrups

Strips of leather called stirrup leathers are attached to the saddle to hold the stirrup irons in place. You will probably learn to ride with safety stirrups which have a special strap which comes undone and lets your foot slip out if you fall off your pony.

21

How to mount a pony

Before you can go anywhere on your pony, you will have to get on or mount it! Follow these steps to learn how. You could even practise doing this on the arm of a chair or sofa if you attach two stirrup irons to a stirrup leather or perhaps a canvas strap.

1 Stand with your left shoulder to the pony's left shoulder so that you are facing its hindquarters.

2 Hold the reins in your left hand above the mane and in front of the saddle.

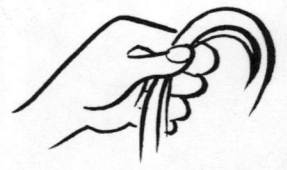

3 With your other hand, turn the stirrup iron so that it faces you.

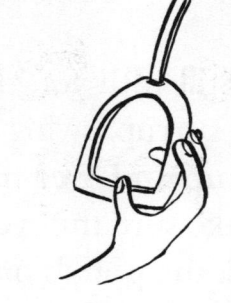

4 Put your left foot into the stirrup and slightly turn your body towards the pony.

5 Still holding the reins in your left hand, reach up and take hold of the saddle.

6 Now gently put pressure on to your left foot and the stirrup as you push up from the ground with your right foot.

7 Still with your left foot in the stirrup, swing your right leg up and over the pony. Make sure that you don't kick the pony's back as you swing your leg.

8 Now sit down carefully into the saddle, making sure you don't come down into the seat with a thump that may hurt the pony!

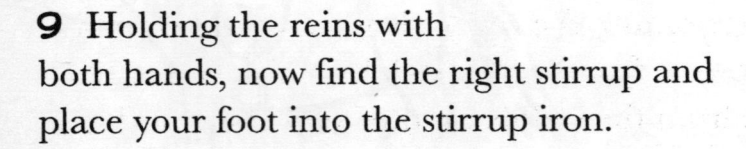

9 Holding the reins with both hands, now find the right stirrup and place your foot into the stirrup iron.

10 Now you've mounted your pony!

Trot on!

Once you are on your pony, you can move forward with him in four ways: walking, trotting, cantering or galloping.

Walking: When you walk with your pony, every stride he takes is the same length and at least two of his feet are on the ground at the same time. A pony walks at about eight kilometres per hour.

Trotting: When a pony trots you will hear its hooves make a "one two, one two, one two" beat because the pony's legs move in two pairs (opposite front leg to back leg). You can either rise from the saddle on the "two" beat and then sit back down on "one" (a rising trot) or you can sit in the saddle for the whole time.

Cantering: Faster than trotting, when you canter with your pony you will hear a "one two three, one two three" beat. This missing "four" beat is when all the pony's hooves are in the air at the same time!

Galloping: This is the fastest pace for a pony and it makes a very quick "one two three four" beat. Some ponies and horses can gallop at seventy two kilometres an hour. You will gallop with your pony when you are very experienced.

How to dismount

It's important to learn to get off or dismount your pony properly so that you do so safely and without hurting your pony.

1 Hold the reins in your left hand.

2 Take both of your feet out of the stirrups.

3 Then take your right leg behind you and swing it up over the pony's back. Make sure that you don't kick the pony as you do this!

4 As your right leg comes down to meet your left leg, your body leans over the saddle like this:

5 Now you will land both feet on the ground. Try and do this without landing like an elephant!

Where to go for riding lessons

If you are very lucky, you might have a friend or a relative who can teach you to ride. But not all of us are that lucky and so need to find a riding school. Look in the telephone book for the names and numbers of local schools or contact your local Pony Club (see pages 43–46 for more information about this) for advice. If you have a friend who is already having riding lessons, why not ask them where they go and if they are happy there?

The Riding School Checklist
1 Is the riding school clean and tidy?
2 Are the stables clean and tidy inside?
3 Are the people who work there also clean

and tidy? Are they wearing the right clothes? (See pages 14–17 for ideas about what they should be wearing).

4 Is there an indoor school which can be used when it is raining?

5 Is there a variety of ponies to suit all sorts of riders?

6 Are the ponies happy and quiet and neatly turned out?

7 Do the riding instructors have recognised qualifications from the British Horse Association?

8 Can you afford the cost of lessons and buy or borrow the right clothes and boots?

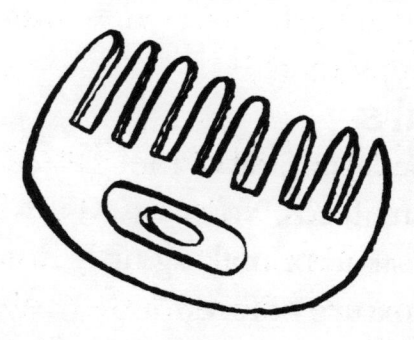

What to feed a pony

We all know that ponies like to eat grass but grass alone is not enough for most ponies that are ridden. Remember that a pony only has a small stomach so they may need up to four small meals a day. Here are some of the different foods that can be fed to a pony. Don't forget that, just like you and your meals, your pony will like the taste of some of them and not the others!

Pony Nuts

These are pellets made of the different pony feeds. You can buy these instead of making up your own mixture of feed.

Barley
This can either be crushed or rolled.

Cooked Linseed
This will make your pony's coat shine. But make sure that the linseed is cooked as it is poisonous to ponies when it is raw.

Apples
Cut the apple into small pieces so that the pony doesn't choke.

Carrots
Again these should be cut lengthways so that the pony doesn't choke.

Hay

Hay is grass that has been cut and dried. Some ponies are fed on hay during the winter when they can't get enough good grass outside to eat. You can hang it in the pony's stable using a hay net.

Salt Lick

Ponies need to be able to replace the salt they lose when they sweat so a salt lick (which is a block of salt) can be kept in their stable.

Sugar Beet

Some ponies are fed this to fatten them up. Others have it to help them digest their other food properly. But it is vital that sugar beet is well soaked in water for two hours before being fed to your pony!

CAUTION! POISONOUS FOODS!

Here are some foods which you should make sure your pony can't eat:

1 Ragwort. This is a plant with a bright yellow flower which looks a bit like a large daisy. If you see it in a field, pull it up so that ponies and horses can't eat it. However, if it has been dried, your pony won't come to any harm.

2 Acorns. Make sure your pony doesn't graze in the autumn in a field which has oak trees.

3 Yew. This can be found in hedges.

4 Bracken. This grows in woodland areas.

5 Deadly Nightshade. This grows in dark, damp places.

6 Unsoaked Sugar Beet. If the sugar beet hasn't been soaked overnight, it will swell up in the pony's stomach and give it colic which is a bad tummy ache.

7 Raw Linseed. Never give linseed to your pony unless it has been cooked.

Grooming your pony

A pony has to be kept clean and tidy so that it is comfortable and healthy as well as smart. If your pony is kept in a stable you will want to groom it every day. Ponies that are kept in a field need to be groomed regularly but perhaps not every day. Always groom when your pony is dry and before riding. This is so that you do not brush all of the natural grease out of their coat and take away their waterproofing!

It is important to use the right things to groom a pony:

A body brush

A metal curry-comb for getting the hairs and mud out of the body brush.

A rubber curry-comb for getting the hairs and mud out of the pony.

A sponge to clean the pony's eyes, mouth and nose.

A sponge for cleaning the dock.

A stable rubber (this is a bit like a tea towel) for giving the coat a final polish.

A comb for combing the mane and tail (but take care not to pull the hair out: if this happens use a brush).

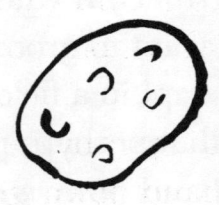

A hoof pick for cleaning away
any mud and stones from the
pony's hooves.

Hoof oil and a brush for
cleaning the hooves.

You will be taught how
to groom a pony at riding
school but here are some tips:

1 Start by cleaning up the hooves. Rub your
hand down the back of one of the forelegs and
then pick up the pony's foot by holding the
front of the hoof. Now start at the heel and
work your way to the toe, picking out the mud
and stones. Do the same with the other foreleg
and then start on the hind legs. Make sure you
always stand with your hands on the front side
of the pony's leg so that it can't kick you!

2 Brush the pony with the body brush starting behind the ears and working down the neck and over the body. Then brush the pony's head. Be careful not to be too rough with your pony and make sure that you comb the curry-comb through the body brush to remove the mud and hairs.

3 Gently brush through the pony's tail, mane and forelock.

4 Dampen the sponge you keep for cleaning the dock to wipe under the tail. You will need to hold the tail to one side while you do this.

5 Dampen the other sponge and wipe around the pony's eyes. Rinse the sponge again before you wipe the nose and mouth.

6 Finally dampen the stable rubber and wipe it all over the pony's coat in the direction of the hairs to make the coat glossy.

Remember! You should always approach your pony with care and kindness. Never rush up to a pony screaming and shouting. Talk to him quietly and calmly and always be gentle when you handle him. Treat a pony the same way you would like to be treated yourself!

Mucking out and stable stuff

No one wants to live in a dirty house and neither does your pony! Ponies can't do the vacuuming so it is up to you to look after your pony and make sure his stable is clean and tidy. So put your wellingtons on, grab a wheelbarrow and a four-pronged fork and get mucking out.

First of all pick up all your pony's droppings with the fork and put them in the wheelbarrow. Next push the clean straw to one side of the stable and make sure there isn't any dirty straw underneath it. Once you are certain that you have cleaned away the dirty straw, take the wheelbarrow to the muck heap and dump all the dirty straw there.

Using a sturdy yardbroom, sweep the floor of the stable and place any further dirty straw into the wheelbarrow for taking to the muck heap. Now leave the floor to dry.

When you are happy that the floor is dry, lay fresh bedding on the stable floor. Make sure it is deep enough for the pony's hooves not to scrape along the floor. You will also need to make sure that the straw is deeper at the sides of the stable so that the pony can help itself to stand up if it lies down.

Now you should go outside the stable and tidy up the yard area before finally providing your pony with fresh water and a meal.

Once you have led your pony into its stable, make sure that it is securely locked in. Remember a happy pony is one that is clean, tidy and well-fed!

The Pony Club

Joining your local Pony Club is a great way of becoming really involved with ponies and to make pony-mad friends. The Pony Club was originally founded so that other people just like you could learn to ride and enjoy all kinds of sport connected with ponies and horses. Here are just some of the activities that you could take part in when you join a Pony Club:

Pony Club Camp

These are run during the school holidays. On a Pony Club Camp you will go away for at least one week to live, breathe and sleep ponies! You will usually stay in a tent or a cabin with all of your friends — and the ponies will be stabled nearby. At the Camp you will get the chance to learn more about ponies and their care. You will take part in lessons to help improve your riding skills and learn more about looking after the stable and your pony's tack. There will also be pony treks where groups of you will go off riding for longer distances than usual. And, of course, there will also be lots of games for you and your pony to play which will teach you more about riding and be great fun at the same time!

Lessons

Even when you are not at Pony Club Camp, your local branch is there to help you learn more about your pony and how you can improve on your own riding skills. Lessons are run by volunteers who can give you the benefit of their own expert riding and pony skills.

The Prince Philip Cup

Every branch of the Pony Club has the chance of entering a competition to win the Prince

Philip Cup. Branches take part in a series of heats where they play mounted games which show off their pony skills. The final of the competition is at the Horse of the Year Show which is held at Wembley in the United Kingdom. The winners have to work very hard to beat the tough competition from the best pony riders there are!

Gymkhanas

Apart from the Prince Philip Cup, the Pony Club also organises gymkhanas where Club members get the chance to compete in the show ring against members of other branches. These are another chance to have great fun and to see how well your own riding skills are improving!

How to find out more

There are branches of the Pony Club all over the world although the Head Office of the

Pony Club is in the UK. Each branch is run by talented volunteers and there is a district commissioner who coordinates all the branches in one area. If you have a friend who is already a member of your local Club, why not ask them to take you along to their next meeting? Or you could contact the Head Office:

The Pony Club
The British Equestrian Centre
Stoneleigh
Kenilworth
Warwickshire
CV8 2LR

They will put you in touch with your local Pony Club wherever in the world you live.

Riding etiquette

It is important for all riders to be polite to their pony, to other riders, and to people they may pass on the road while they are riding. Make sure that you remember your manners when you are out riding!

What you wear
Always make sure that you and your pony are wearing the right clothes for the occasion.

● Make sure your pony looks smart and is properly and safely tacked up. (See pages 14 to 21 for more information.)

● Check with the landowner before you take your pony off a bridleway. And never take your pony across a field without asking the farmer's permission first.

● Always leave the bridleway as you found it.

If you have to open a gate make sure you shut it again after you have ridden through it.

If you are riding on the road, always thank car drivers for slowing down or stopping for you. You can do this with a smile and a nod or by raising your hand to thank them.

Use hand signals to make sure that people know what you are doing.

To show that you want to turn right, put your right arm out like this:

If you want to turn left, put your left arm out like this:

To show that you want to stop, put your hand up like this:

If you are travelling in a group of other ponies, make sure you tell the riders behind you that you are intending to stop – otherwise they will ride into you!

🦯 When you are riding on the road, always ride in the same direction as the cars and other traffic.

🦯 Never ride too closely past a parked car. You don't want one of the passengers to open the car door on your pony, do you?

🦯 It is safer not to ride in the dark, but if it is a dark day, make sure that you are wearing a reflective waistcoat or bib. You can also wear fluorescent armbands and put similar bands on your pony's legs.

🐎 When you are riding out, wear a waistcoat or bib which has the words "YOUNG PONY AND RIDER! PLEASE PASS WIDE AND SLOW" written on the back of it.

🐎 If your pony has the habit of kicking out at the back, tie a red ribbon on its tail to warn other riders!

🐎 Remember to thank your riding instructor at the end of every lesson.

🐎 Never enter a show ring before the previous rider has finished and left the ring. Wait until directed by the ring steward.

✎ When you have finished riding, always remember to thank your pony and give him lots of praise!

✎ Remember your pony always comes first! No matter how tired or cold you may be after riding, make sure that your pony is stabled, groomed and fed properly before you think about looking after yourself.

Top riding tips

Remember that however gorgeous a pony is, he is only as good as the person riding him! Here are some things that will help you become a better and more confident rider:

- Never tug hard at the reins. This will pull at the bit and could hurt a pony's mouth.
- Hold your hands down towards the pony when you are holding the reins. You should never hold your hands high like this:

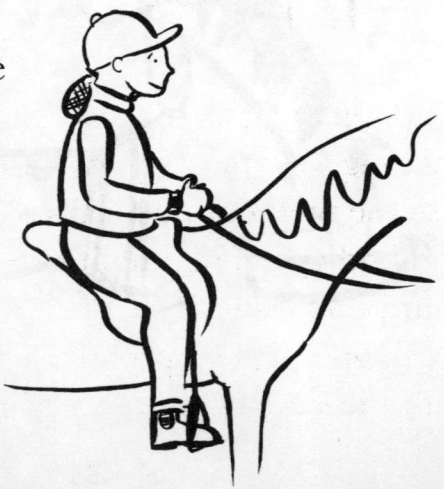

🌀 Always keep your knees in line with your toes.

🌀 You should hold your heels down and toes up in the stirrups like this:

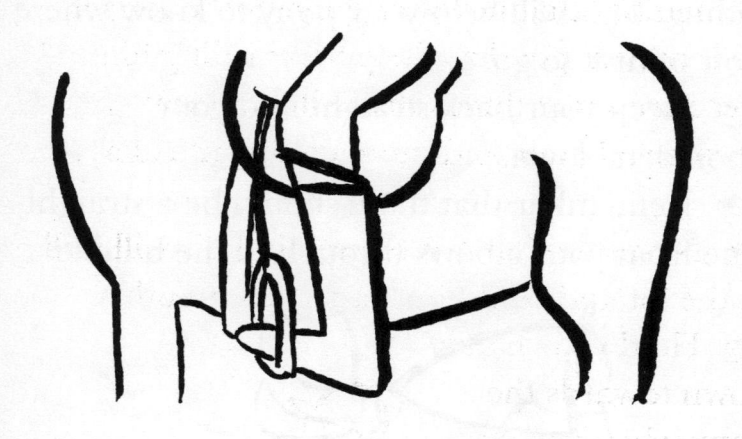

🌀 Don't nag at your pony! Constantly chatting to your pony will only confuse him. Use the methods and skills of using your hands and body you are taught at lessons to control your pony instead.

🌀 Don't hurt your pony! Squeezing the pony with the sides of your legs should be enough to tell your pony that you want it to go forwards. A slow or lazy pony should be gently nudged with your heels.

🎀 Always look in the direction that you are riding. This will help your pony to know where you want it to go.

🎀 Keep your back straight and your shoulders down.

🎀 Remember that there should be a straight line from your elbows through to the bit like this:

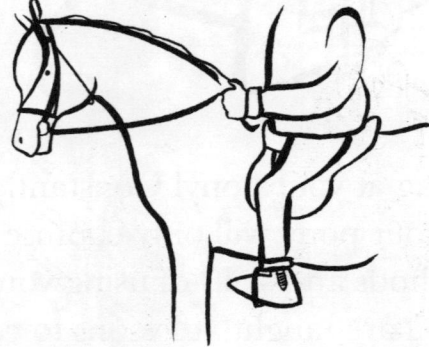

🎀 Once you learn to jump, always remember to praise your pony with a pat when you have jumped a fence.

🌀 Always look towards where you want to land when you are jumping. If you look down you will confuse your pony.

🌀 Never overtake another rider without telling that you are going to do so.

🌀 If you are tense, your pony will be too!

🌀 Always walk the course before you take part in a competition. That way you can discover where the tricky bits are and decide where you are going to start to jump and turn your pony.

🌀 Practise! Keep practising and you will become a better rider.

Gymkhanas and shows!

Gymkhanas and shows are a great opportunity for you to take part in competitions and to discover how much you and your pony have improved. You will find out about when and where they are being held at your riding school or from your local Pony Club.

Gymkhanas

You need to be a confident rider who rides a plucky pony to really get the best out of a gymkhana. At a gymkhana, you will get the chance to play mounted games with your pony, often competing directly with lots of other riders or as part of a team. There are all sorts of games and competitions including:

Apple Bobbing

A bucket of water has an apple floating in it and you and your pony gallop towards the bucket. You have to dismount and try to grab the apple with your teeth before mounting and galloping back to the start!

Litter Race

A variety of "litter" is placed across the paddock — things like cardboard boxes, plastic cups and items of clothing. You have to try to ride around the paddock and pick up the "litter" from the saddle by using a cane. You cannot finish until you have picked everything up!

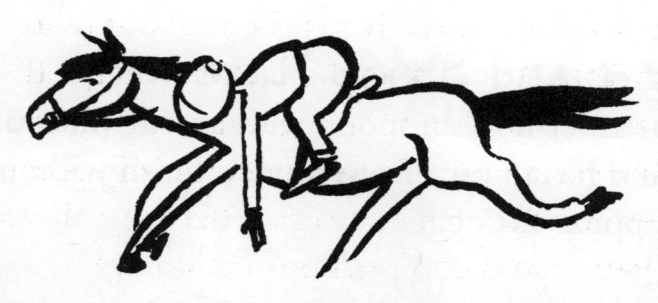

Saddling Up Race
Saddles are placed all around the paddock. You have to ride your pony bareback and dismount before gathering up your saddle, saddling your pony up and then mounting and galloping back to the start.

Balloon Race
Two balloons are attached to a post midway along the paddock. Another two balloons are fixed to a post at the far end of the paddock. You have to ride to the far end and grab a balloon, return to the middle post and grab another balloon and then gallop to the finish without losing a balloon!

Egg and Spoon Race
The rider holds a spoon with an egg placed in it and has to race from start to finish without dropping the egg!

You may also be asked to take part in races where you need to bend down from the saddle, see who can trot the fastest, or arrive at the correct points of a compass.

At a gymkhana you might win prizes for your individual skills or for taking part in a winning team!

Shows

Your riding teacher will be able to advise you about which classes are suitable for you and your pony to enter. Even though you will be entering as an individual rather than as a team with other riders, always remember that you and your pony are a team anyway — you can't do anything without each other!

A show pony should always be fit and expertly turned out so it should be:

- Well-groomed and have its tail and mane pulled or plaited.
- Have its hooves oiled.
- Have a shiny healthy coat.
- Have polished and correct saddlery.

A show pony's rider should be:

- Wearing the right clothes (see pages 14 to 17).
- Be neat and tidy.
- In smart polished boots.

Always acknowledge the judges when you enter the show ring.

When you enter the ring in a group of other ponies, you should do so at a walk. After the judges have looked at all the ponies, they will then ask you to "trot on". During this time, the judges will be looking carefully at all the ponies. Next you will be asked to canter and again the judges will be scrutinising the ponies. Finally you will be asked to take your pony back to a walk before stopping.

The judges or the ring steward will then ask

or "call in" the ponies that they like the best.
These ponies and riders will be asked to show
off their skills individually. They may be asked
to make a figure of eight at a trot or perhaps
do a short canter before coming back to stand
in front of the judges. The pony will then be
asked to go back into the line with the other
ponies whilst each of the chosen ponies does an
individual show.

After all of this, the ponies may be stripped
of their saddles and then the judges will
examine the ponies' confirmation (which
means their bodies). Finally, the ponies are re-
saddled and mounted and ridden around the
ring again at a walk. Rosettes are usually
awarded for first, second and third.

Other Show Classes

As you progress with your riding skills you may
be asked to enter showjumping classes where
you compete over a course of different jumps.

You may also take part in fancy dress competitions where you and your pony are dressed up for a theme. In some classes, prizes are awarded for the best turned out ponies or for the best of a breed. There are also classes for girls to ride side-saddle which is when the rider does not sit astride a pony but rides instead like this:

Many years ago when girls very first started to ride ponies, all girls were expected to ride side saddle as in those days they only wore skirts and never trousers!

You've won a prize!

If your pony has been placed in the top five, you will be called out of the line by the ring steward or the judges. Sometimes, rosettes are awarded for all five of the ponies and riders but often there are only three rosettes. If you have won a rosette, you will be asked to walk your pony further forward and then a rosette will be placed on your pony's bridle by the judge. Congratulations!